TWENTYSOMETHINGS

by

Janae J.

Printed in the United States of America.

ISBN-13: 978-0-578-78035-1

table of contents

Dedication

Dedicated to the twenty-year-old in you and me.

I'm giving you my heart. The quiet places I've run to om 22 until 29. I'm giving you the tears I cried during heartbreaks and seasons of depression/anxiety. In these pages lay the ever changing path to my healing. I want nothing in return. You can ave all of me. My only hopes are that you too heal through these words. If healing doesn't occur, I pray you find understanding. I ray you construct a new world within yourself. A world that has lors of hope, love, joy, and deep healing. You are worthy of it. You leserve it. This has been my therapy. Sharing these moments is a part of my journey.

Icebox

creating a relationship with you feels odd...
like 1, 3, 5,
the 2 of us just don't add up
like the back and forth in double dutch
i ain't ready yet.

You are my biological father,
Part DNA on paper,
But...

i don't know you.
i don't trust you.
i don't know how to.
-stranger in my home

there was a story I created for us
a compensation for the things we
i mean you lacked.
you were you but you know
better
who I wanted you to be
i was i but you know
the same
unwilling to change
probably why the abyss only grew wider
probably why I continuously blamed you for childhood drama
you didn't know any better
you did and loved the best way you knew how
past trauma lingering in your dna
no one is to blame
just know
I love you
i pray you don't take this the wrong way
-Dear mama

my mistakes brewed the anger in you
erupted the muffled malice you had
blow after blow you spewed
let it all go
upon my back
across my face
gripping my arms to stay in its place
-child abuse

wrote it all in my notebook
backtracked when it was time to confess
practiced multiple conversations
noted every outcome
but for some reason
i couldn't let you in
when it counted
i lost my voice
-temporary paralysis

i set a picnic for death
anticipated his arrival
i knew he would come sooner or later
so I waited by the pond
until dawn

the sunrose
and life showed her beautiful face
birds sang
butterflies gave flight
children played

and yet I waited for death
too afraid to live a life worth living
-fear of flying

be gentle with me
i am *fragile*

it feels like a constant ritual of playing the blame game
always finding self in the shoes of victim
holding on to past hurts
old scabs still oozing with pus
refusing to find home in skin again
a world lost in translation
repeating negative incantations
inherited by the worldly view of self
the things you say to your body
and mind
resembles hatred
-acts of self abuse

procrastination is a childhood friend
i've been trying to shake her
since i could pronounce her name
whenever productivity shows his face
here comes her ugly ass
in hand with my phone
netflix and chill
don't forget Jack Daniels
a text from my ex
a 30 min nap turned into 2
i hate that bitch

-bff

Tap into me

Deflate me

Because I've been holding my breath for far too long

I'm suffocating at the tension of my mind's anxiety

Make me burst

Create a safe space for me in your place

Where I can let go

Pop every emotional trauma I've held close

Locate the truths

Help extinguish the falsies

Give me the means to coop

Not escape

I want to

I need to

Face every dark corner I've neglected to embrace

Because not every dark space needs to be expelled

They too need acknowledgement

They too wait for compassion

Gentleness

Grace

-A note for my therapist

i've taken left turns
in the wrong direction to avoid you
sweaty palms grip the steering wheel
heart up to throat
knowing I have nothing
in the trunk
on my person
it's just I'm afraid
even when I know I've broken no laws
top notch American citizen
abiding by every rule and regulation
i'm weary cause I could still get lynched
i can still be haunted like a wild animal
in my 29 years of existence
i've never seen on my news feed
black male guns down white man while jogging
with no arrest
but for some reason
when you get behind me
blue causes my anxiety to stir
red my blood rushes to the surface
sirens resemble the cry of my mama if you was to shoot me
like they did all the innocent before me

i have ptsd

inherited through the bloodlines of my ancestors

caused by your inability to see my skin color
as worthy of human rights

i've been trying to heal

but you

mr. officer and your repeated offenses
don't seem to want my best interest

probably why I decided to leave

the great states of America

i can't fathom raising my seeds

my sons

my daughters losing their loved ones

at the hands of your distaste for our melanated skin

yet, you've profited off of the hardships of my kin

you've poisoned entire communities

burned down towns

with the audacity to call us lazy and unable to fend

our entire culture has been worshiped and repurposed

sold to the fashion and music industry without our say

but when it's time to take a stand for the very people
who have fed your children

where are you?

where are the marches and protest?

dear America,

i think you've gone in the wrong direction

as I look in the reflection of my driver's side mirror

i pray, Lord please don't let this officer pull me over today

now he's going to mistake my mental disorientation as hesitation
which makes him nervous

intimidated

it seems we have developed the same mental illness

fear birthing fear

unwilling to acknowledge the historic pain

that has led us here

in my avoidance

i go the opposite direction

now I'm 20 minutes late for work

all because of the rapid replays of innocent blacks

killed by the guns held

by the boys in blue

-inherited ptsd

growing up
my body seemed to be at the forefront
flat booty
longs legs
fairly thin
it began at home
followed me to school
Like a stray dog
making its home inside my head
barking incessantly
mocking my anatomy
i hated the teasing
i hated the body God thought fit
and sooner than later
i hated myself
-self abuse

seeing you blossom
while I was still a sprout
triggered me
brought out the worse
in me
covered in malice and jealousy
i stunted my growth
blocked the sun
from giving me light
too focused on the tulips
neglecting the sunflower
that was being produced
inside of me

-jealousy

i see you,

i see your hurt,

i see the scars from being unseen

scars that have turned calloused

i see you,

i see your despair,

i see the tears churning into anger

outlined in violence

i see you,

i see your soul

wrestling within so patient and willing,

waiting for the day you let go of it all,

those pains are not your name

those scars are not your fame

-to be seen

how bad would it be,
if we all communicated how we really felt?
-don't lie to me

i don't know when it began
maybe in elementary
i started to run
hide
shelter myself
become small as possible
in hopes of not being seen
deep desires of wanting to fit in
brick by brick
letting no one in
created a persona resembling the world's copy
i swear I hated her
hated myself for continuously playing dress up
attempting to be everything to everyone
buried myself and now I miss her
and now I can't find her
but I'm looking
-identity crisis

I cannot offer what I do not have
do not ask

You don't own the rights to my story
-don't plagiarize me

It's a delicate thing,

evolving.

It hurts,

separates,

and brings you to some truths

your ego never really wanted you to face.

It's scary shit you know,

growing up,

finding the real you

after years of being what the world

wanted.

-finding neverland

Heartbreak & 808s

i still remember the day they locked you away
your sister and I walked the halls
filled them with prayer
holding on to tears
fearful they would cause a tsunami in the courtroom
you stood there
big black and unarmed
yet they feared you
deemed you unfit for society
son father friend and lover
we knew we lost
my expression pale
Unaware this was the end
the straw that broke the camel's back
-goodbye my love

i still play the highlight reels of our love story
sometimes I let others watch
i tell them the tales of our adventures
the wild young love
every girl dreamed of in her teens
you gave me my favorite gift
the greatest love story of my twenties
every ounce of us was a rush
until we crashed hard
face first
still holding hands
and each other's hearts
-fast and furious

i devoured your love
always wanting seconds and thirds
needing you to be present at all times
like babe on nipple,
in your absence
i became empty
wishing to be full again
scratching in addiction
resemblance of feen,
my bones cling to my skin
i won't eat until your presence meets my gaze again
what is this bad love you've given me?
what is this exchange we've agreed upon?
your love for my freewill?
i don't recall signing on the dotted lines
it's too late
you've become a parasite
leeching on my heart
i've become a host
to ignorant of my demise
-addict

like the pages of a good book
i licked my fingers at each page
devoured the words
i needed more
until I fell upon the final chapter
i gave those pages more time
attentively
savoring
every punctuation
exclamation point
-waiting for the sequel

I dream of you before
I
fall
asleep.

i won't say I miss you
but the experience of loving you
still lingers in my bed
-daydreaming of you

she needed love
and you knew that
your resume said "knight and shining armor"
dressed up your words to undress her
then left her naked
unkept
she mistook you for love
she added you to her dictionary
love is:
when true love shows it's face
she will never know it's real name
-real love

my heart isn't broken
i'm just mourning our relationship
pay me no mind
i'll be fine in a month or two
-situationship

i think the veil is finally lifting
things are finally starting to melt
connect
no more reading in between the lines
forthright discussions exposing feelings
love seems to have a hold
rose colored glasses for every occasion
i think the veil is finally lifting between you and I

-honesty

all my exes are still in love
the *fantasy*
dances in their subconscious
interactions far
near
bring them back to the moments
sending their hearts
their mind
their sacral chakra
back to me
-feminie energy

how many times have you stayed?
you knew there was nothing left
but you belittled your self worth
feared your growth
so you stayed in a place void of substance
void of love in your language
sacrificing your own season to flourish
how many times did you stay?
he left you home with a bottle of wine
tears to caress your face
and when he came home at 6 am
with a lie on his tongue
perfume on his collar
you still stayed
you still stayed
how many times?
-know your worth

pains me to say no
when you look into my eyes
i see our memories
our sex
hands lost and finding their home
amongst breast
down spine
finally on ass
sheets a mess
throats parched
it was missed
i won't lie
but enough is enough
you were never mine
-boundaries

love me the way god intended

that's all I ask

do you love yourself?
are you healing from your trauma?
are you aware of the hurt
subconsciously acting in your absence?
-*first date* Q&A

this is it
the drift before the rift
silent treatments
and empty texts
when we part the I love yous lose their luster
our relationship has losts its worth
In each others world
we've become strangers
i'm not sure if i care anymore
when we finally end
i pray it feels like we never met

-strangers

the memory of betrayal slips into my mind
whenever i smell your fragrance
i hear the music that was playing
i relive the exact moment
you were wearing gray sweatpants
your long dreads were tied in a ponytail
gathered by one of the rubber bands
you so often wore on your wrist
your feelings walked away from me
nonchalantly
i tried to twist them back to me
futilely
and yes
i say I have forgiven
but have I?
If i repeatedly
choose to explore the pain
the guilt
has justice been served?
are we both living in a repeated past tense scene?
our wounds wide open
our healing not insight
and the jury is still out on deliberation
-my heart needs justice

let's not be afraid to do it over and over again
fall and then get back up
again
let's not be so desperate to protect our hearts
that we forgot to give
when the right one appears with arms
ready to receive
our love
responsibly
-trustworthy

i've learned to not ask permission
to give what I have
if you receive it
good
if you desire not and walk away
okay
in the end my purpose was met
i gave what I had
-i loved while I could

sometimes I stare at you
frown between eyes
deep in thought
reach my hand out
are you real?
fingerprint to skin
lips to collarbone
prefrontal cortex on mute
inhibition lost
i am all yours
have your way with my love
-once upon a time i fell in love

anticipated your calls
did you forget I exist
checked inboxes
no messages
dry like sand
did you lose my number
maybe I should call...
-pick up the phone

i sat in silence,
it's not that I had nothing to say,
i was just hoping,
your curiosity for me
exceeded behind what you could see
-i hate second dates

i wrote you a love song,
erased every line,
scribbled down I hate you instead,
crossed through it,
i didn't mean it
but this pain
deep in my chest
rising through my neck,
I gotta get rid of,
let go of,
the feeling of failure
because we didn't make it
-thin line between love & hate

i loved you in every lifetime
let's get it right this trip
around the sun
before we crashed on this earth
in this realm
we made a promise
to push and pull
finding balance within our polarities
yin and yang
you provoke the ugliest parts of my humanity
forcefully encouraging them to die
for the betterment of I... us... the whole
-karmic relationship

love me
like it hurts
to be

a   part

love should be big
not quiet
nor misguided
direct
to the point
like exclamation
not a question mark
or any ordinary sentiment
possibly a few run ons
conjunctions connecting our spirit
holding us together
accompanied by ands yets untils
cause i want to love you until
the end of time
endless
timeless
love should be an action word
sprinkled with adjectives
addressing my two favorite pronouns
-you and I

don't think I've learned my lesson with you
test the waters but I'll always jump in
fools rush in
blind lead me blind
leave me dumb
leave me numb
leave me wanting more
love, you've got some shit with you
i'll accept it every time
shovel it
sell it like it's gold
my drug of choice
you're high is the highest of highs
got me needing to feel all the feels
don't think I've learned my lesson with you
And I don't want to
-i need rehab

no need for alcohol
or medicinal marijuana
you take me there
and bring me right back
-high on you

i wanted everything to work out

wanted you to be happy

so I fought

i mean I ran

made it look like I put up a good fight

but in the end

i was the coward

too afraid to stand

too afraid to say when

when it was the end

i led you to the grave

took the long way around

hoping I could pretend

as if the roses were in full bloom

they were dying

i held a veil against your eyes

you didn't see it

premeditated murder

but...

I love you

-i swear

when you leave my presence
i wish you nothing but the best
every lesson learned
every I love you held close
when you leave my presence
may you walk away on higher ground
let it lead you back to the highway of purpose with no detours c
distress
I hope your confidence grew in my world
your passion for life was ignited by my touch
it stirred your need to be more than what you could see
i wish you nothing but the best
when you leave my presence
even though I won't be a part of your future
no animosity will be gained
the love will be the same
i wish you
nothing
but
the best
-Sincerely

i created space
you wanted closure
i didn't have it in me
it was fun while it lasted
let's leave things before we have to end it
-swipe left

i gotta love jones for your love
all up inside of me metaphorically
metaphysically I feel thee
need to be where presence goes
near your bones
in your zone
no caution
i'm full throttle racing
racing to your love
down by your side
for your love I'll cause wars
slay dragons
deliver the heads of giants
down on your luck I'm the charm
wear me around your neck
i'll be your protection amulet
i'll be whatever need be
just look my way
Mr. Stranger
on the third stool by the bar
-pick up lines

i don't want your now

if

i

can't

have your forever

I love you without expectation.
I give you space to be,
to explore every person you choose to create.
I pray you will do the same for me,
because the face you see today
will become many before I pass away.
-unconditional

quite frankly,
i'm over writing love letters
but it's the only thing
churning
dancing
seducing my subconscious
i need it
i want it
to give
and be
loved.
-we all want

last night I ran to my dreams,
i leapt head first in,
melting quickly into slumber,
hopeful you will make an appearance
like when we first met,
i forced memories to the surface,
stealing fragments of emotions,
the passion we held,
the fire all consuming,
nothing left in the furnace,
only   ashes   of   what   once   was
-memories set ablaze

somehow I knew you were everything I needed

but not anymore

dreams deferred stirred in my bones

pleading to fly

i ignored

my heart became sedentary

unwilling to move

for I loved you

you became the only matter

my soul cried for years

i ignored

until the universe took you away for a season

a flood came sweeping me into isolation

i prayed endlessly

god, "what the hell is this?"

soul whispered

find the blessing in isolation...

dig deeper into self

find the dreams once deferred for love

find you

find purpose

love will come again

but

not

now

-not now

i had you
at my doorstep,
in our home,
on my fingerprints,
you were my definition,
my values included your name first and last,
so when you left,
things shattered,
walls crumbled,
my city caved in,
i caved in,
chest to lunges no air
and these tears kept tumbling down,
the nights felt endless,
and when mornings came I couldn't bare them
no one knew,
i just couldn't tell them,
i visited our favorite locations to feed my comfort,
only to end up feeding my tears,
at the bar with jack to intoxicate my feelings
and deep sorrow to sober my soul, p
ainfully coming to the realization,
i lost you.

-ex

emotionally unavailable was the label
woman, you do not have to wait
but believe him when he says
emotionally unavailable
don't trick yourself
into his bed
nor his head
-lord send me a sign

i've changed my mind
about you
about us
my ways aren't the same but you
you've been unchanged
stuck
and I have to leave
i cannot allow
this to hold me here
i must go
you may stay but I must
go
-outstayed my welcome

i used to want to get married
ya know,
diamond rings
big wedding bells
ballroom gowns
tuxedos and chandeliers
Now,
i just want authentic love
hearts full
spirits aligned
the two of us creating
and formulating a new world
the ones left behind can fully enjoy
-*what i really want*

the way you look into my eyes before a kiss
feels like breath before death.
daily,
i plead to live once more,
only to die again in your arms
via your lips.
-ready to die

with me,
you don't have to pretend.
-pinky promise

you expect me to trim my hair
while yours grows
wild like flowers in a field
i think not
trim yo shit before you enter my box

-manscape

i won't swim deep for your love
i won't even wade in the shallows
for your love
you must understand
i have overflows
waterfalls
of love pouring out of me
so if it should be
i have to risk it all
to make acquaintances with your love
i'm good love,
enjoy
-not worth the cost

Love Letters

hold with care,
this side up,
please lift from here,
instructions on how to carry me

inside this human body
contains a fragile ego
made of glass

i've grown to appreciate her delicate ways
she makes me aware
i observe her,
i acknowledge her,
her and I often exchange ideas
we create realities in different worlds
transforming dark galaxies into star lit milky ways

she's been bruised and abused by many
and I assure her,
it's never personal,
people all over mother gaia
are learning to coexist
with the fragile glass like ego within
-handle with care

I whispered to self...

ɔw to love you, through toxic mental noise creating toxic actions
nd relationships.I vow to love you in times of healing enclosed
ı solitude. I vow to love you when no one is watching and when
it becomes a spectator sport. I vow to reside in places where
authenticity lays its head.

-*until death do us part.*

does a caterpillar question its purpose?
build upon the anxiety and anticipation of becoming
i wonder...
does it have days of deep depression and lack
consumed by the opinionated opinions of other caterpillars?
probably not...
-probably not

i don't feel it always

the need to put together the image

the facade

or attend the dress rehearsal

in hopes the audience will like my performance,

therefore,

i don't.

i won't.

anymore.

who cares?
opinions and thoughts are just that
none of your concern
be as big
be as fragile
as you choose
this world will be less
without you
authentic you
before mom gave name
before world bestowed shame
you were perfect
you are perfect
-*don't hold back*

i measured my worth in accolades
i couldn't seem to measure up
weighing myself esteem in others' measuring cup
i wasn't sure which metrics to use
the worldly views
the opposing cues
or my own indication of success
nevertheless
in conclusion the former never seemed to matter
nothing ever seems to really matter
once your atoms no longer exist
in this realm
of myths and fables
-legends never follow the crowd

i'm

not

asking

for

permission

-self validation

the rhythmic pattern of formulating words
calls me like ball to player
small glimpses of clarity
climb from the ventricles of my heart
digging deep into my skin
until pen meets paper
fingers kiss keyboard
with every word my spirit lifts into dance
forming a lyrical contemporary explosion of thoughts
Guided by soul and heart

-passion

to be as a plant
silent and patient
humbly growing with no need of an audience
climbing towards light
maneuvering away from darkness
digging deep into soil
taking only what is required
-nature is the teacher

what if this isn't real and we've all forgotten

the purpose of our creation

to create

to love

brainwashed that pain and angst is the only reality

It is not

Wake up little seeds

It's time

Grow

Sprout

Bloom

Reach for the light

It's the only way out

And into freedom

-escaping the matrix

i wonder if human lives matter in other galaxies
i wonder if black and white coexist in different realities
i wonder if other worlds have found their peace
i wonder if they think earth is ghetto
sometimes I do
often
i wonder
-spaceship conversations

i fellowshipped with the sun
found joy when the moon rose in its place
knowing all things are temporary
knowing each day will be new
with a new sun
and a new moon
-all that matters is now

you've been given everything you need
from the time you were born
til the day you leave this place
life is happening for you
not against you
-silver spoon

i decided to do my makeup today
i walked down my neighborhood
"Ms., you look pretty today"
went to my job
applause and stamp of approval
had a glass of chardonnay
by the bar
marina view
your husband was charmed by the sight
you the same but you'd never say
crept back to my home
removed the mask
eyelashes
lipstick too
took a view in the mirror
barefaced human
baby,
you are golden
the cosmetics are only an additive
to your cosmic presence
enhancing the flourishment of your blossoming garden

-inner beauty

they called themselves grasshoppers
compared to giants
when all along
they too were
giants
-comparison minimizes

everything has an expiration date

ideas

friends

lovers

opportunities

everything must go for things to be new again

-8.15.19

People are drawn to you. Your laughter. The way your smile reflec
the light of the sun. Your assurance in self gets them high. They fe
your magic before they even know your name. You've been to th
lowest of places. Climbed to the highest of mountains. Held han
with God just to be who you are today. Never let the misaligned
steal the magic you worked soul hard to create.

-*you are the light*

the silence welcomed her in
in my meditative state she made her home

my lungs became her bed
as she rested her head
my breathing grew deeper
shoulders sank into relaxation
eyes gave away obligation
to see through foggy lenses
and false pretenses

and here I lay
above the clouds
atop the mountain top
of my spiritual awakening
-cultivating symbiosis with peace

sometimes I cry,
it feels so good to be alive...

reflect
be still
surrender
take each problem
each suffering
each duty
moment by moment
never rushing to meet 2 before 1
-*awareness*

we forget our parents are humans
we forget their lives were theirs before we became
with veiled eyes we see them as golden
never tarnished by the world's pollution
-adult ephipany

teaching pulled me from myself
forced me to mature before the options were given
24 little humans
on the edge of their seat
waiting for my magic
they anticipated my every move
studied each habit
transforming all my energy
little alchemist
big dreamers
i owe my twenties to you
-mother of many

take a step back.

be proud of all the work you've put in.

it may not feel like it now but baby,

you have come soul far.

-the journey

learn something new...
how to love you
void of environment
circumstance
and false narratives
undress the avatar
it's tired and worn out
sit down with the true self
close your eyes
find the stillness between inhales and exhales
and remember to be gentle
shower yourself in grace
bathe yourself in love
-you deserve

every season comes with its duty
renewal
truth
blessings
contemplation
learn from each
they hold the key to your salvation
ignore the lesson
and the cycle will continue
until you become a master of self

My greatest fight has never been with those consisting of flesh and bones but with my inner thoughts. These thoughts wrestled with my soul, targeted my nervous system, and created anxiety that rose up to my shoulders. The world weighed on them. I was unbeknownst of ways to relinquish the pain until you came with your cognitive therapy and coping skills.

-black therapist matter

my first love was my sisters
dressed in their 90s cool
wrapped in black beauty
i loved
i watched i admired
ti'l this day I do
-first love

you deserve

moments of deep clarity

baths filled with rose petals and essential oils

silence met with hidden whispers of enlightenment

vulnerability clothed in empowerment

secret I love yous told to self when depression tries
to show her intolerable face

authentic relationships that build your soul
because you've done the soul work

you deserve

truths

love

joy

and abundance that last beyond human form

-*worthy*

Dear women,

You are the beginning. You are the end. What is for you will alwa·
be. Take the time to heal. To be everything you need. Don't rusł
the feels. Breathe. Take all that you need without fear. Become.
Whatever you need will appear when you are ready..

-*perfect alignment*

i walked on water just to see if the story was true,

it was,

found a mountain

asked it to move,

it did,

used my thoughts in hopes to create,

what a wonderful world I see,

spoke my existence into existence

here I am,

gave,

now I have

i let it all be

and it was

-No pressure

she embraced it all with grace
knowing life's secrets hid not in the obstacles
but danced within the small moments of gratitude
she found them in the stillness of day before sky met sun
through tunnels of meditation given daily for self medication
deep baths sprinkled with Epsom salt and lavender
clearing self of toxins was her favorite recipe
rituals and prayers
love and self awareness allowed her to vibrate higher
therefore she embraced it all with grace
-Don't panic

The statement "I'm not trying anymore" doesn't have to be a negative connotation. It simply means, I've surrendered to what is and what will be. My job isn't to fight against the current. My job is to go with the current,assist in its waves and ride the wave until I find my way peacefully back to the shore.

-ride the wave

some days I choose to conquer,
but this day has swept past me,
lulled me into a trance,
i accepted it,
i relished in the sentiment of doing nothing,
being nothing,
needing nothing,
and living in this consistent new form of *now.*
-your presence is a present

t's ok to claim wanting to be loved. I'm not sure what happened to us...we've become so afraid to say we want and need to be loved. 's natural. It's spiritual. It's a humanistic quality. Stop trying to be a hard rock when you really are a gem. You deserve to be loved. I ow you want to give it. So give,without fear. It may come or it may o but either way give love a chance. What a shame it would be to live a life without experiencing love in its totality.

-it's ok

give yourself what it needs

water

time

love

nourishment

listen to your soul as it yearns to go further

while you're stuck in between worlds

acknowledge your feelings but don't hold on

they will never stay

get out your own way

what is

will be

-always

you've been through a lot
somehow you're still here
living past survival

you've done it. you are doing it.
soul work: a constant cycle of death and rebirth.
winter, spring, summer, and fall
even trees give way to the falling of leaves,
the loss of what once felt complete
to give way to what is necessary for today,
may we all be brave,
brave enough to live to die and be born
again

-born again

i've lived in many places
despair with roads laid in insecurity
anger hidden in valleys of hut
fear climbing heights taller than skyscrapers
i've been to many places that led nowhere
-i refuse to go back

lean into me
i am safe
i will hold you up
when your limbs give way
and muscles become fatigue
i am here
-sisterhood

dear parents,
let go of the fears,
let your children live,
release control,
you have none,
they will grow and be,
make room,
show them the path without force,
ignite their passion,
dismiss your desires,
they will be who they will be

i was told to always have high expectations
so I did,
when failure came knocking
as it does,
my feet stuttered at each step
unable to redeem myself
repeatedly I created these notions
for self and others,
repeatedly I got knocked violently down
only to discover,
expectations are like the weather channel,
a whole lot of educated guesses
never knowing the final outcome
until it happens
*-or **doesn't***

the cramps are creeping in
i give way
exhaling and inhaling
refusing relief by medication
i let mother nature have her way
naturally
body takes care
shedding the unnecessary
replenishing my wo(mb)manhood
healing and never taking

-*new moon*

Dear truest of self,

I love you for holding on. You've climbed out of sunken places w
such grace, my mind cannot even fathom. At my weakest, I thou
you were gone. I thought you were fed up, packed your bags, a
asked God for a new home. So I prayed and I cried out. "Show
her, build me to be the person you intended." Against deep wav
high climbs on treacherous rocks he led me your way. There y
were, so peaceful, so at ease with the sway of our hips, the curve
our spine, no care for validation from the world.

-thank you

I am releasing the past
while honoring the lessons,
I am surrounding to the present
thankful for each breath,
I am manifesting my future
knowing all things work for my good.

-*morning mantra*

and then there is you...
an expression of God
potentiality
written poetically within your DNA
you will and will always be
a masterpiece
i pray each day
you see
possibility
gratitude
and ways to create
a better world
transformed by every
thought
action
conceived
by and through
you
-note to self

acknowledgements

I cannot express enough gratitude to the people who nurtured
my growth during my twenties and now.
Thank you to my parents Joseph and Lisa for allowing me to fumble
but never fall. I want to give a humongous thank you
to my two second moms, my big sisters, Denisha and Erica. I'm not
the woman I am today without the watchful eyes
of my younger courageous sister, Chantel.
Lots of hugs and gratitude to the women who have listened
to my tears and held me close.
Thank you to all the boys who broke my heart in the most
perfect way leading me to love myself.
Thank you to my therapist, Marc Hardy for showing me how to find
clarity through the noise.
Last but definitely not least, thank you a billion times over to Dawn
Michelle Hardy, The Literary Lobbyist.
Without you, this book would still be a google doc
on my google drive.

to my readers

I can't believe it's finally here! You are amongst one of the FIRST people to enjoy this book.

As a self published author, I take pride in knowing the people who support me will spread the word. Therefore, I have a small but homungous task for you. Are you up for the job? Here's what you can do to help TWENTYSOMETHINGS reach the masses:

1. Take a picture (or video) of you when you first lay eyes on the book and tag me **@luvjanaej**. I'll add your picture to the highlight section TwentySomethings First Look on my Instagram page.

2. Send in a brief reflection of the book. I'll add it to the SheaButter Publishing website on the Readers Reflection page.

3. Tell any and everybody about the book; email, blog, tweet, Instagram! Be sure to tag me and use the hashtag #twentysomethings

4. Post a positive review on Amazon once the book is available for sale.

5. Buy a couple of copies for your family and friends.

Be creative! Have fun! All positive ideas are welcome.

Thank you for your support!

SheaButterPublishing.org
Instagram: luvjanaej

about the author

Educator and poet Janae J. was raised in Raleigh, North Carolina. She describes herself as a spiritual being having a human experience. Janae works as a first grade teacher in Abu Dhabi, the capital of the United Arab Emirates. Twentysomethings, her debut poetry collection captures the raw and ever-changing emotions experienced by young adults who are navigating first heartbreaks, self-doubt and figuring how to show up in the world. When she is not engaging on social media or enjoying the works of poet Rupi Kaur she is educating herself on best health and wellness practices women of color.

IG @luvjanaej

www.shaebutterpublishing.org

Made in the USA
Columbia, SC
26 November 2020

25579474R00070